Beyond the Hidden Veil of Shame

ONE WOMAN'S POSTABORTION JOURNEY
TO A SETTLED AND PEACEFUL HEART

Kay Hall

WESTBOW
PRESS®
A DIVISION OF THOMAS NELSON
& ZONDERVAN

WestBow Press books may be ordered through booksellers or by contacting:

WestBow Press
A Division of Thomas Nelson & Zondervan
1663 Liberty Drive
Bloomington, IN 47403
www.westbowpress.com
1 (866) 928-1240

ISBN: 978-1-9736-8951-5 (sc)
ISBN: 978-1-9736-8952-2 (e)

Library of Congress Control Number: 2020906906

Print information available on the last page.

WestBow Press rev. date: 04/30/2020

CONTENTS

Dedication vii

Dear Reader.. ix

Chapter 1   Acknowledgment 1

Chapter 2   Facing the Shame 13

Chapter 3   Acceptance.......................... 23

Chapter 4   Reflection............................ 33

Chapter 5   Forgiveness 41

Chapter 6   Grace.................................. 53

Chapter 7   Redemption.......................... 63

Resources 73

About the Author 75

DEDICATION

To my mom, who loved me through all the tough times in life and would always reassure me that "This too shall pass." She was there to celebrate the good times with her beautiful smile and welcoming arms.

I love you, sweet heavenly momma.

DEAR READER

Although I can't address this letter personally to you, I know we have a common bond. That bond is the desire to move toward a healing from a decision we made long ago. This workbook is designed for you to really study your heart. It's purposely more workbook than words. It's meant for you to journal in, think deeply about, and move into your own healing.

Throughout the book you will find scriptures that speak the truth, and you will find questions that will challenge you. This is your journey, but I pray that you first sit quietly and ask Jesus to come into your heart and walk through this workbook with you.

Ask Jesus to go back to those places in your heart that hurt, that are numb, or that you have just blocked off. Identify what He shows you, and journal the grace He gives you. You are not alone in this, even if you have never shared with anyone about your abortion. Jesus is with you. He really is. He has no judgment on you. He's waiting for you to turn around and run into His loving arms.

I began this journey feeling the same way that you may be feeling right now. I thought it just might be easier to go on living like it never happened. Like it was another life, another time. Well it's not. It's real, and it happened.

What I also found was that how I feel today can't even compare to how I was feeling. I am free, filled with hope and joy that healing is more real than the abortion. I am strong and courageous because I gave this all over to Jesus to heal and renew.

This journey began when I was asked to do a video for a local ministry. I realized that if I was going to put myself out into the world as a postabortive woman, I needed to be a postabortive woman who was seeking forgiveness, grace, and redemption. I began to seek ways to challenge myself and move forward into a healing grace.

I needed to tell my family what I had done. Well that was game changer for sure. Tell my family, what, why. Lord? Yes, my family needed to hear it from me, not from social media. If you're at that point, I'm here to testify you'll be surprised at the outcome. I speak to this later in the book.

With each chapter, start off with your heart in prayer. Take your time. However long it has been that you have lived behind the hidden veil of shame, this workbook is designed to take you beyond the veil of shame to live a blessed, healed life. All with God's blessing and assurance that you are loved, you've always been loved, and you'll never be without His love.

CHAPTER ONE

Acknowledgment

The first step in any healing is to acknowledge what you experienced and to have the desire to move through the pain into forgiveness and healing.

GOD'S WORD

I acknowledged my sin to you and my iniquity I did not hide I said I will confess my transgressions to the Lord, and you forgave the guilt of my sin.

Psalm 32:5

To begin, let me tell you how my journey started. At a women's retreat, I asked Jesus to show me my life, to make it clear to me what it has looked like behind the veil of shame. What I saw was bleak. Dark. Without life. Picture this: A playground where the toys that once gave delight to children on a warm summer day were all rusted and broken. The soft green grass that welcomed little bare feet was dead, and the fence that once stood to protect the playground was broken and rotting. The sun that once sent its warm rays to wash over the playground was distant and dark. That was my life, my life with shame. It's where I had chosen to set up camp. It was empty and void of any hope or light. It was where I needed to be to start the journey back. I needed to acknowledge my life as it was after the abortion.

Now take a moment and reflect on your journey back. The following questions are here to help you draw out the story within, and to help you sit and ponder what the Holy Spirit will reveal to you.

All these questions are meant to help you acknowledge the abortion and what was evolving at the time in your heart. There are no right or wrong answers in this workbook. They are *your* answers.

Dig deep into your memory and acknowledge where your heart was at the time. It can be very frightening to acknowledge those feelings, those moments we went through. However, tremendous healing will surface when you come face-to-face with your heart.

TIME TO PONDER

Your journey beyond the hidden veil of shame begins here.

1. Think back to the first time you understood what an abortion was. What did you feel?
2. Think back to when you decided to have the abortion. What did you feel?
3. Think back to when you walked into the abortion clinic. What did you feel?
4. Think back to when you walked out of the abortion clinic. What did you feel?

SPEAKING TRUTH INTO YOUR LIFE

I am God's child.

I am beautifully created.

I am Christ's friend.

I am accepted.

I am clothed in His righteousness.

A PRAYER FOR
YOUR HEART

Father, You have given me the courage to face what has for so long been the chains that bound me to my sin. I am grateful that this bondage is not where You want me to be. I know that You want my heart to be free, free to love again. I start by loving You. Your only desire for me is to be free and to break the chains that weigh so heavily on my soul.

I give You this moment and every moment to follow to mold my heart and give it new life.

As I take this journey, Father, I ask for Your continued protection and presence. Let nothing stand in my way. The battle is Yours, but in order to know the power of Your love, I need to be present to see Your glory ignite.

I trust in Your plan for my life. I know that You continue to pursue me through every step. Father, I believe You have a perfect plan for me, and I submit to that plan.

My actions in the past do not define my path for the future. I am not what I have done, but I am who You say I am: beloved, courageous, loved, one with You in the spirit, fully healed, and clothed in a white robe. Your princess, Your child, and I love You, Lord Jesus.

JOURNAL PAGE

JOURNAL PAGE

Your joy may be shaken, but
it will never be stolen.
Khall

CHAPTER TWO

Facing the Shame

If we avoid identifying the shame and live a life filled with regrets from the past, our future will continue to elude us.

GOD'S WORD

For I will be merciful toward their iniquities,
and I will remember their sins no more

Hebrews 8:12

For so long shame controlled my heart. It left me without hope, worthless and stuck.

I saw what I had done as what I was and always would be. Shame became my go-to place when I was down. I would place shame on my soul like a coat in winter, covering up the sin and not dealing with it.

Do you ever have something that concerns you and just continue to deal with it? It might be financial, physical, emotional, or spiritual. Day after day you're reminded of this nemesis. You start to give yourself excuses such as, "When I win the lotto, I'll never need to pay another bill," or, "As soon as this headache goes away, I'll be able to feel like myself again," or how about, "I should feel bad about the relationship I'm in because I never seem to say the right things." You may even have thoughts of, *I'll never be as good a Christian as the other person because I've never read the Bible.*

All these excuses keep you in a holding pattern of life. Picture this: A pilot is on the runway, ready to go. All systems are in place, and the tower has given the pilot a clear runway. Yet he just stays in a holding pattern. The tower repeats its clearance to take off, but the pilot doesn't move. Knowing his destination, what is holding him back from pressing into the throttle and taking off? What does he see that the tower doesn't? Junk on the windshield. Junk that will not have any affect on his ability to fly. You see, for so long I kept seeing junk on the windshield.

God in His infinite wisdom sees the big picture and gives us clearance to fly. But we choose to focus on the junk on the windshield and stay on the runway. It's time to trust in our Lord and Savior in the tower and fly. It's time to trust in His vision and direction to take off.

TIME TO PONDER

1. What is your definition of shame?
2. How does that definition align with what God says in His Word? Do a search for all the scriptures about shame. You will be amazed at how many there are.
3. If you knew back then what you know now, would you have done what you did? I bet your first reaction is no. So, what does that say to you about who you are today?
4. What does living without shame look like to you?

SPEAKING TRUTH
INTO YOUR LIFE

I am sound-minded.

I am an overcomer.

I am forgiven.

I am seated with Christ in the heavenly realm.

I am complete in Christ.

A PRAYER FOR
YOUR HEART

Father, shame can grip us and blind us from the truth that You give us in Your Word. Peel off its grip and take off the blinders that hold us captive. Rescue us, Lord, from our own selves that continually bring shame into our hearts. Defend us from the evil that seeps into our souls.

I pray for the one reading this, Lord, that shame will fall away as the winds of the Holy Spirit blow softly over her soul. Give her reassurance that she is whole in You, and nothing can separate her from Your love and protection.

JOURNAL PAGE

JOURNAL PAGE

God, help me to see me like you see me.
Khall

CHAPTER THREE

Acceptance

Accepting the past as it is, separating sin from your soul, opening your heart to receive God's grace

GOD'S WORD

So now there is no condemnation for those who belong to Christ Jesus. And because you belong to him, the power of the life-giving spirit has freed you from the power of sin that leads to death

Romans 8:12

Acceptance of who I am—just me, myself—is a difficult thing to grasp. I'm a sinner with faults. It is easier for me to condemn myself than it is to focus on the good that I bring into the world. It's because I was stuck on the things I've done in the past. All the wrong decisions, the wrong actions, and the godless life I once was drawn to.

I didn't see me as God sees me. Without fault. Forgiven. Desired. Pursued. Captivating. His creation. His child. So why, if such a great God can see me like this, can't I? Why is it easier to fall into the ditch and fumble around in a world of very little self-love? It's because I truly can't imagine how I can be loved when I did such an evil thing, have an abortion.

Can you relate? Right now, as you're reading, are you feeling what once was in my heart—despair, self-hate, unworthy, without value? I'm sure you can add to this list.

We need to see ourselves as Jesus sees us. Accept ourselves as we are accepted by God.

How do we do this? With the help of the Holy Spirit. Seriously, our inabilities to accept that we have sinned and accept God's forgiveness is as simple as saying, "I believe Jesus died for my sins and that I am a child of God. I am protected and loved."

Think about this: You are a creation of the Creator of the universe. If He loves you, then how can *you* not love you? He created you. Not accepting who you are is to say, "God, You made a big mistake when You made me." Not possible. Are we still sinners? Yes. Does God still forgive us? Yes. Can we accept the things of the past and believe that we have been forgiven? Yes.

TIME TO PONDER

1. What part of you do you need to accept and move on into full surrender of your lack of acceptance?
2. Given that your head knows you're forgiven, how will you work toward moving that into your heart?
3. Write and ask the Holy Spirit to show you where you need to surrender any self-hate, despair, and lack of confidence in the gifts you have received from the Lord.
4. When you have thoughts that you're unacceptable, ask yourself, "Is what I am thinking true, and if it's not, what is the truth?"

SPEAKING THE TRUTH

I am peaceful.

I am free in Christ.

I am free from all fear.

I am Holy Spirit-controlled.

I am healed by the stripes of Jesus.

A PRAYER FOR YOUR HEART

Heavenly Father, there are times when things are just not all that clear to us. Times when we know the truth but find it difficult to comprehend. Give us wisdom to understand, courage to trust, and faith to believe.

I pray that while this beautiful woman is seeking acceptance, You give her a word of truth and encouragement to know how much You truly love her and will never leave her side. Guard her heart as she pursues the truth that You truly love her and see her as Your loving daughter.

JOURNAL PAGE

JOURNAL PAGE

In the valley or on the mountaintop,
the only difference is the perspective.
You are the same. Just as beautiful
as strong, as valuable as loved.
Khall

CHAPTER FOUR

Reflection

Today I am a mom of six, a grandma of fifteen, and a great-grandma of three. I'm a professional life coach, a chaplain for the Billy Graham Rapid Response team, and am married to an amazing man who has given me support throughout my journey. Normally happy endings come at the end, but for this story, I'm starting off the beginning with where I am today, sharing the hope that waits for everyone.

My life has had many challenges along the way. Some came with an easy solution, some with a lesson, and some with long-lasting impact.

When I was sixteen years old, I gave birth to a baby girl. She was a beautiful baby, but I was in no position to care for her; nor were my parents. With the lack of ability to give my baby girl the life she deserved, I gave her up for adoption. It was a hard and painful process to walk into a courtroom and sign her away, even though I was convinced I was doing the right thing for her best life. It didn't take long before I went back to a life of sexual freedom because that was where I felt loved. I felt that if I gave of myself, I would be accepted and loved, if only for a moment.

I met a man, and our time turned into what I thought would be a long-term relationship. I wasn't expecting what happened next. I became pregnant, and his response was, "No babies." Faced with the woundedness of my teenage pregnancy, I decided I was not going to go through this alone, so I went to the abortion clinic and had an abortion, alone, frightened and terrified of what I had or would become.

The cold and lifeless room of the abortion clinic left my soul chilled and empty. The smell of the sterile instruments was nauseating. The sound of the equipment used would echo in my head for years and years. To manage through this vortex, you place your life in tomorrow. It's literally impossible to be in the present at such a time as this. The coldness, the smell, and the sounds created memories of horror. For years this imagery was buried deep in my trail of wounds.

Reflecting on the vision that Jesus showed me at the retreat of what my life had become, I asked God for forgiveness and to move my life in the right direction. Repenting of the sins of my past, I was given yet another glimpse of the playground. Far in the distance was an image of Jesus restoring the toys on my playground. He gently cleaned them and made them new. His message was that He would do this to all my toys—my wounds—in the playground and would restore the grass to a beautiful green. He would mend the fences to put protection around my life. He was restoring my life because I asked for forgiveness. He was giving me grace and redeeming my soul.

Why this passion to reach out to women who have had abortions and those who are considering abortions comes now is a mystery to me. My message to those who have had abortions is this: Healing is a desire. Pray for that desire. Healing won't happen without acceptance of God's forgiveness. Grace is the ultimate gift. Receive it. Redemption is freeing. To be redeemed is to be free from shame. Bringing this wound into the light of our Lord is necessary for dismantling the continuous badgering from Satan.

My message to those considering an abortion or those who feel trapped and that an abortion is the only way out it to consider this: Your time in the abortion clinic may only be minutes, but the effect of what you are doing will be embedded in your heart for a very long time. I can speak to you from experience about adoption and abortion. With adoption, you carry your child to birth and give it into the loving arms of one who will care for your child. In an abortion you carry your child for a short time and then give it to a machine to be discarded. In both pregnancies, this is your child, and you carry this child. But only one child makes it to live a life as deserved.

There is always a beginning, middle, and an end to each story. I started my story in reverse because I want to give hope to those whose hope is slowly fading. The beginning of forgiveness, grace, and redemption is available to you. It always has been and always will be.

JOURNAL PAGE

JOURNAL PAGE

Some days it's hard to know if it's the end
of a journey or just a new beginning.
Either way, your beautiful self has
so much value, grace, and ability
to embrace each moment.
Khall

CHAPTER FIVE

Forgiveness

Forgiveness is knowing that your sin is not a character flaw but an event. It's saying to yourself I am not my mistake. I am whole and healing.

GOD'S WORD

If we confess our sins, he is faithful and just and will forgive us our sins and purify us from all unrighteousness.

Romans 8:12

I am sure the previous scripture is very familiar. What I didn't realize is how important it is to our healing.

> For if you forgive other people when they sin against you, your heavenly Father will also forgive you. But if you do not forgive others their sins, your Father will not forgive your sins. (Matthew 6:14–15)

Think about the scripture above. It's saying something that is very important. If you forgive other people when they sin against you, your heavenly Father will forgive you.

It recalls something else that is very important: forgiving ourselves. We can work through that Jesus has forgiven us, but we might find it tough to forgive ourselves, to forgive our decisions to have an abortion. It's a place we try not to go because it's so painful to first accept our decision and then get to the point of forgiveness. We may hold ourselves in this prison as punishment for our actions. We feel that we don't have any right to forgiveness for our actions. We might feel that forgiving ourselves is a way to say it was all right to have an abortion. We might feel that it may dismiss our actions as just passé.

Lies, lies, lies.

Forgiveness is in your heart. You are saying to the Lord, "I realize I have committed a sin, and I never want to do that again. I'm asking you for forgiveness and for protection over my heart in the future.

Let me try to explain what forgiveness looks like to me. It's understanding that what you have done is not who you are today. If I asked if you would have an abortion today, would you answer yes? I doubt it. Think about this: You have a different heart. You made decisions based on where your heart was at. This isn't excusing the sin; it's accepting the sinner. You see, knowing Jesus and accepting His forgiveness are because you know in your heart you would never make the decision to have an abortion again. You need not continue to keep yourself bound to the sin.

Forgiving myself for the actions I have done in my life seems to be the most difficult. Forgiving others is much easier.

Forgiveness is saying your debt has been erased from my heart. I no longer hold the note on this debt; it's gone. So why do I continue to hold the note on my own debt.

Let's look at this from my heart's view. At the time I became pregnant, I was not able to raise a child; nor was there any support from the child's father. I was alone and felt the only choice I had was to put this pregnancy behind me and move back into a lifestyle free from having any responsibilities.

My mind was made up even before I arrived at the clinic. I was already to tomorrow. I had blacked out what was really happening as though it was a bad dream.

I drove by myself to the clinic and went into the procedure by myself.

Where do I start to weave my way through forgiveness? Is it at the point when I chose to be sexually active? Or at the point when I didn't use protection? Or now, when I drove to the clinic. Maybe the fact that I was numb the whole time of any feelings about what I was doing. Maybe I needed to forgive myself for the sense of relief I had once it was over.

I think forgiveness is a hard sense to identify, but I know for sure that I have because I have no shame. Am I ashamed of my actions? Absolutely. At that time in my life, my choices were not in line with God's plan for my life. I was outside His will by a long shot. I didn't care about His will because my will was getting me where I needed to go. Or so I thought.

When shame goes, forgiveness and love fill the void.

TIME TO PONDER

1. What does forgiveness look like to you?
2. Do you still see your actions as part of your character or part of your story?
3. Can you separate the two?
4. Sometimes when we let go of the shame and forgive ourselves, we are still stuck. Identify where you are stuck and then how you can move out of that position.

SPEAKING TRUTH
INTO YOUR LIFE

I am God's workmanship created for good works.

I am confident to come before God in prayer.

I can do all things through Christ.

I am a treasure.

I am protected.

A PRAYER FOR
YOUR HEART

Father, thank You for forgiving the one reading this prayer. Thank You for sending fresh wind into her soul to confirm Your love. Thank You that You will never leave her nor forsake her through this journey. Be close, Lord, so close she can feel Your heartbeat and know that heart beats for her.

JOURNAL PAGE

JOURNAL PAGE

Perfection is not part of the human
DNA, so how can we expect it
from ourselves or others.
Forgiveness,
Grace,
Redemption.
Khall

CHAPTER SIX

Grace

To ask for grace is a humble recognition of the sin in your life, a belief that you are not your sin, and a desire to move forward.

GOD'S WORD

However, I consider my life worth nothing to me, my only aim is to finish the race and complete the task he Lord Jesus has given me the task of testifying to the good news of God's grace

Acts 20:24

I have spoken about the vision of the playground throughout the book. This is where grace comes in. In that story of such a bleak picture of my life far in the distance, there appeared an image of a person picking up the toys and cleaning them off, renewing and restoring them to their original state and purpose.

That is what Jesus was doing in my life. He was the healer of the wounds represented by the broken toys. He was the restorer of my playground, making it a safe place to play again. He was the fence builder, my protection, grass grower, my joy, toy restorer of my wounds.

Grace became my shield. Grace became my protector. Grace become my salvation. Grace became the bedrock of my faith. Undeserved yet given.

TIME TO PONDER

1. What is grace?
2. How have you felt the grace of Jesus in your life?
3. Have you felt the grace of Jesus in your life?
4. How do you envision your healing?
5. Take Jesus back to your woundedness and ask Him to show you His grace. How does that feel?

SPEAK TRUTH INTO YOUR LIFE

I am forgiven.

I am accepted.

I am loved.

I am free.

I am the daughter of the King.

A PRAYER FOR
YOUR HEART

Lord Jesus, we try to capture the thoughts of Your grace being given so freely but can't even fathom what that must be. To love us so much that You took our sins and died for us. What is that, Lord? How does anyone love that much? Well You do. You love us so much more than we have the capacity to understand. Thank You, Father, for seeing our hearts filled with love for You. Thank You for covering our sins and casting them far, far away. Thank You that we don't have to live as victims but as victors. Thank You that right now You are holding us and protecting our new hearts.

JOURNAL PAGE

JOURNAL PAGE

In all the universe there is no one like you.
No one.
You are part of this plan with purpose.
You add value.
You are a gift to many.
Celebrate you because you
are worth celebrating.
Khall

CHAPTER SEVEN

Redemption

To redeem is to cash in on what you have been given through the cross. You turn in your sin for your salvation. You redeem the old you for the new you.

GOD'S WORD

I have swept away your offenses like a cloud, your sins like the morning mist. Return to me, for I have redeemed you

Isaiah 44:22

Let me give you one last vision of hope. People who know that I have had an abortion often say, "Your baby will be waiting for you in heaven." That statement sends me running, feeling sick to my stomach. How could a baby that I aborted be waiting for me with loving arms? How could that baby even want to see this horrible person?

I'm sure many of you have heard that same consoling statement. Until recently, it wasn't consoling for me at all. The last person who said that to me included in her remarks the fact that heaven is where we will meet, and in heaven, there's only perfect love, no condemnation. For the first time, I could stand still and not run. I could understand that yes, I will see my baby, and yes, we will be reunited in glory. Then the most beautiful image came to my heart. Angels were standing in line at the abortion clinics, gently taking the babies to heaven and placing them in God's loving arms. Is it biblical? I don't have that answer. Is it God's loving heart reaching out to comfort a woman needing forgiveness, grace, and redemption? Yes.

TIME TO PONDER

1. Think about the word "redemption." To redeem, hand over. What does redemption look like?
2. Why do you feel redemption is critical in your life now?
3. Do you accept that you have been redeemed?
4. If not, what is standing in your way?
5. If so, how will you live a redemptive life?

SPEAKING TRUTH INTO YOUR LIFE

You are sealed by the blood of Jesus.

You are filled with grace from Jesus.

You have been redeemed by the love of the Lord.

You are no longer a slave to your past but a victor to your future.

You have been forgiven.

PRAYER FOR YOUR HEART

Father, this is the beginning of an awakening to what You have given us. Keep our hearts full of Your love, our minds clear of any wrong thoughts, and our desire to know You more in every cell of our bodies.

Take this journey, and know You have forgiveness, grace, and redemption in the holy and mighty name of Jesus.

JOURNAL PAGE

JOURNAL PAGE

When the journey you're on changes,
it might be time to enjoy the view.
Khall

RESOURCES

NIV Bible.

Captivating, by Stasi Eldridge.

Grief Share grief recovery support group.

Defiant Joy, by Stasi Eldridge.

Voiceless Movie, written by Pat Necerato.

ABOUT THE AUTHOR

Kay Hall
Founder Kay Hall Ministries
Kayhallministries.com

Kay Hall has her certification as a professional life coach and is currently completing her master's degree in Christian counseling through Light University. Light University is the top-ranking international life coach and Christian counseling university.

Kay also is a public speaker, bringing encouragement through her own experiences. She is the author of *Beyond the Hidden Veil of Shame: One Woman's Postabortion Journey to a Settled and Peaceful Heart,* a book/workbook for postabortion care.

Kay is certified through the Bill Graham Rapid Response Team as an emotional and spiritual chaplain for disasters both nationally and internationally.

Kay is a lifelong learner, certified in lean office simulation, foundations of leadership, developing emotional intelligence, and train the trainer. She also holds a degree in business administration.

Along with continuous learning, Kay brings years of experience to her coaching ministry. She has lived life knowing that each experience brings growth and awareness of the strength she has within.

Printed in the United States
By Bookmasters